TWO

Written by Sarah Tatler

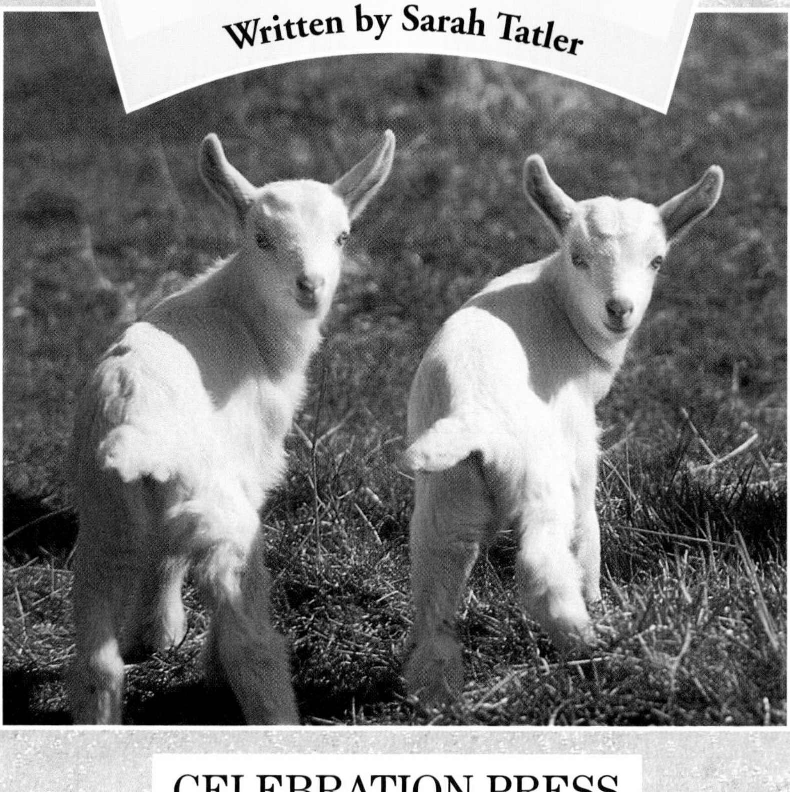

CELEBRATION PRESS
Pearson Learning Group

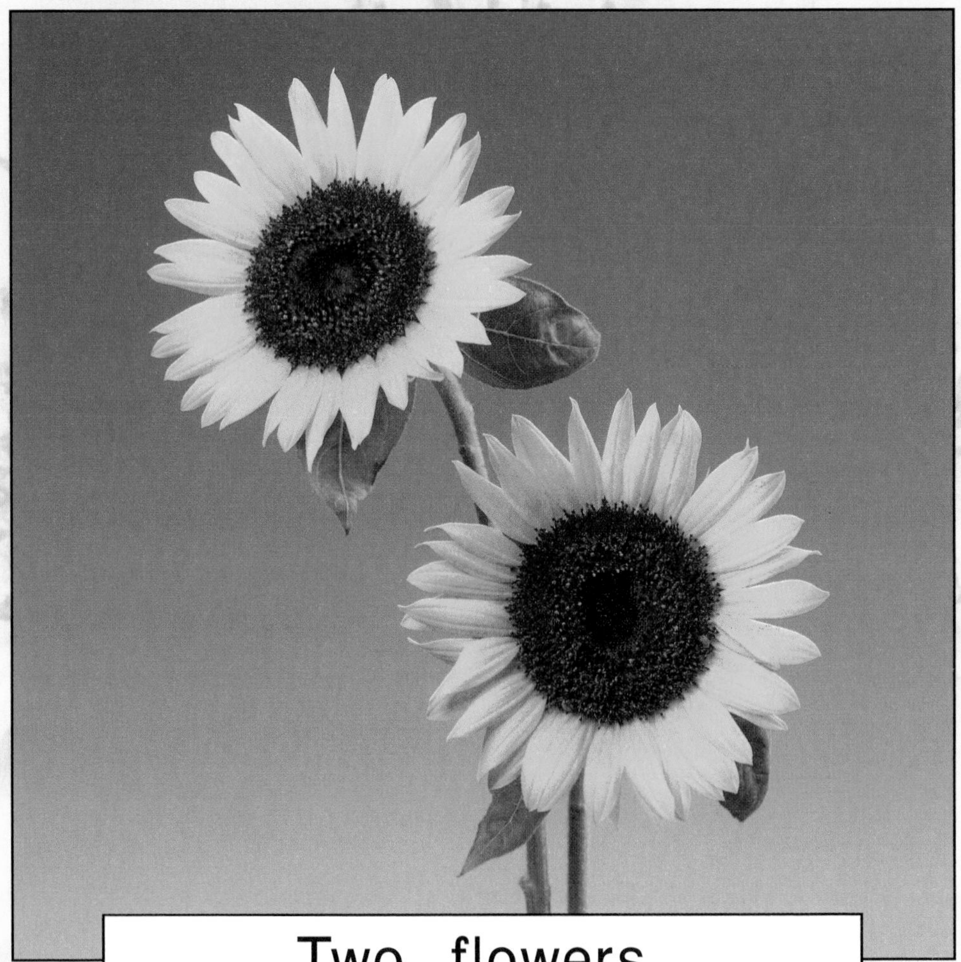

Two flowers.

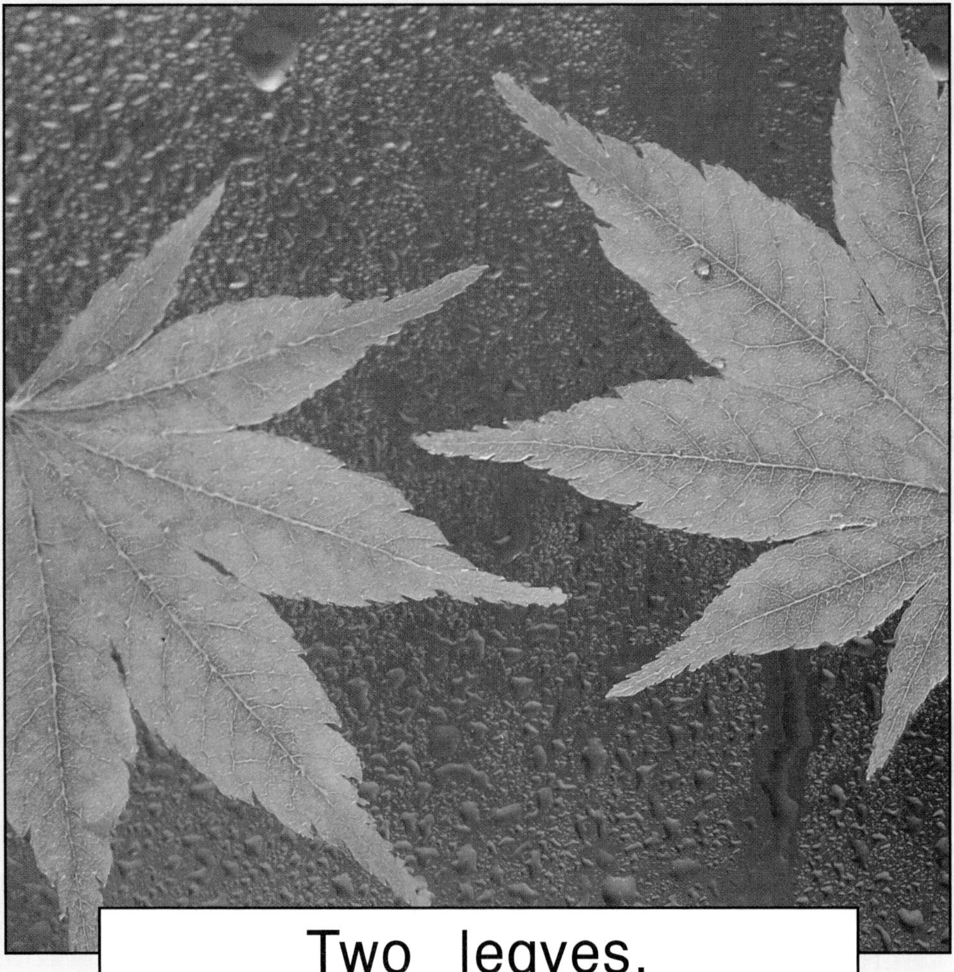

Two leaves.

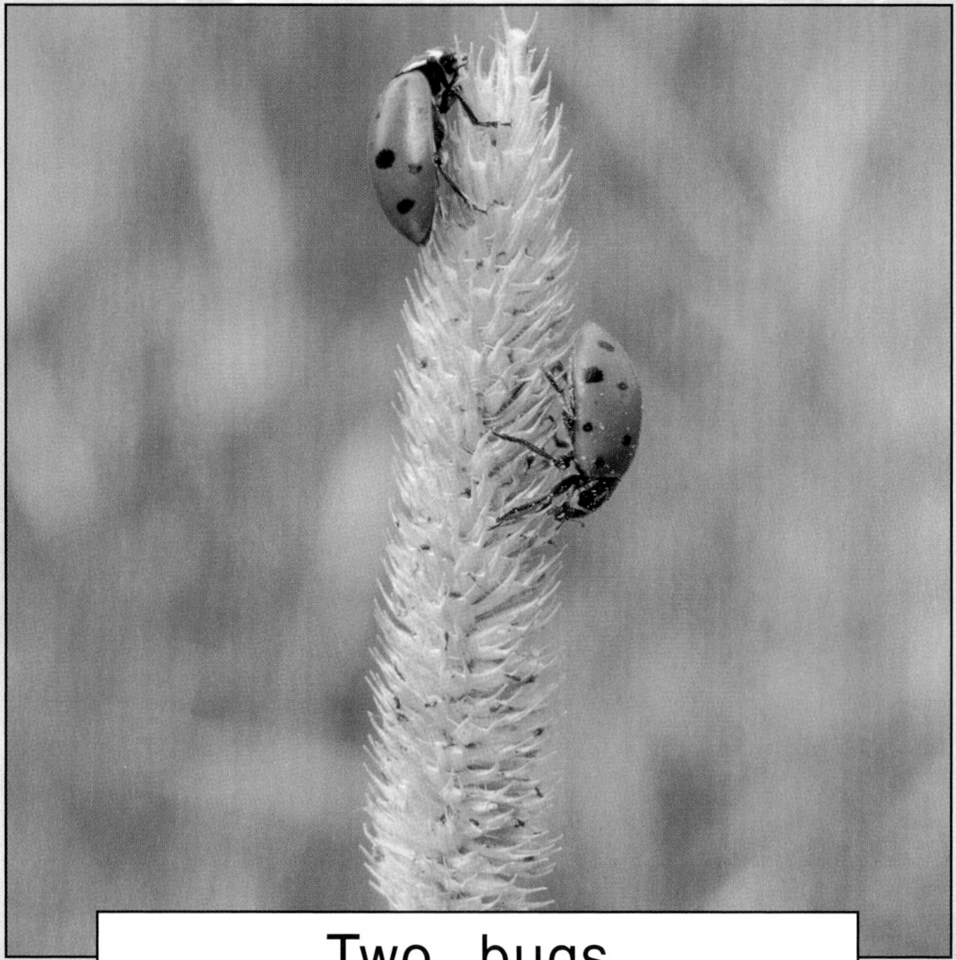

Two bugs.

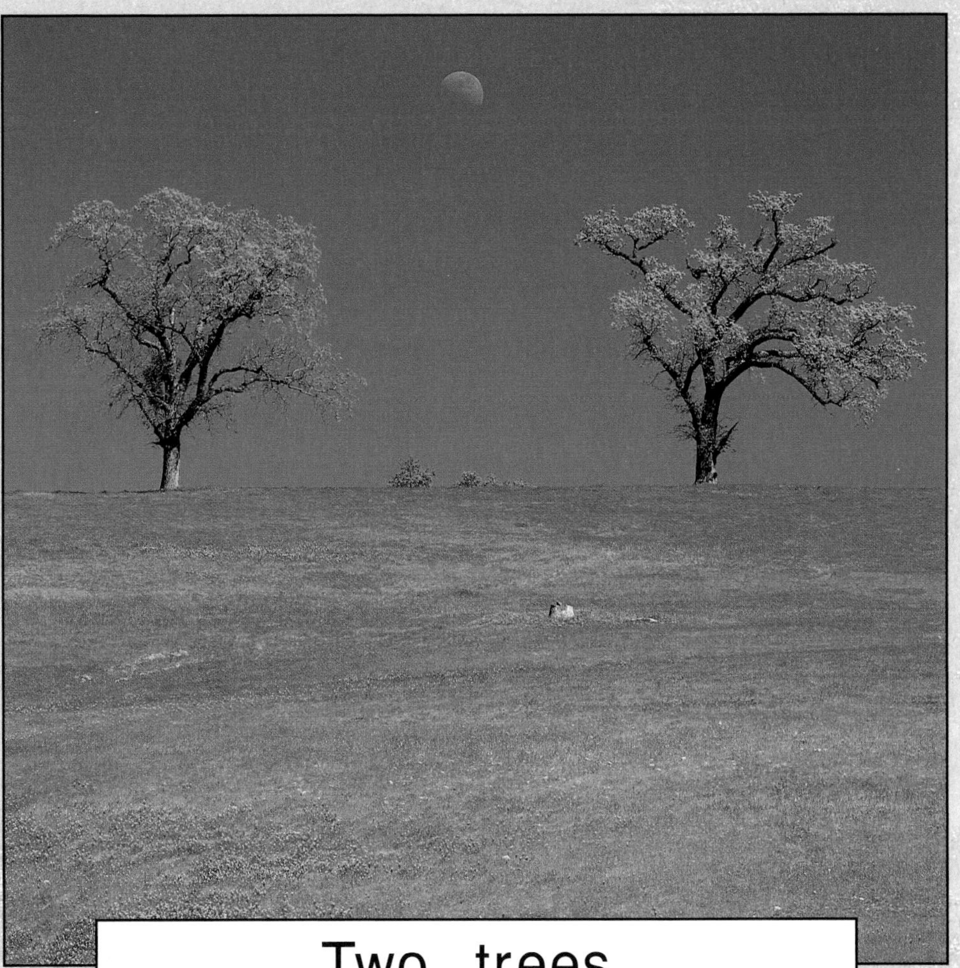

Two trees.

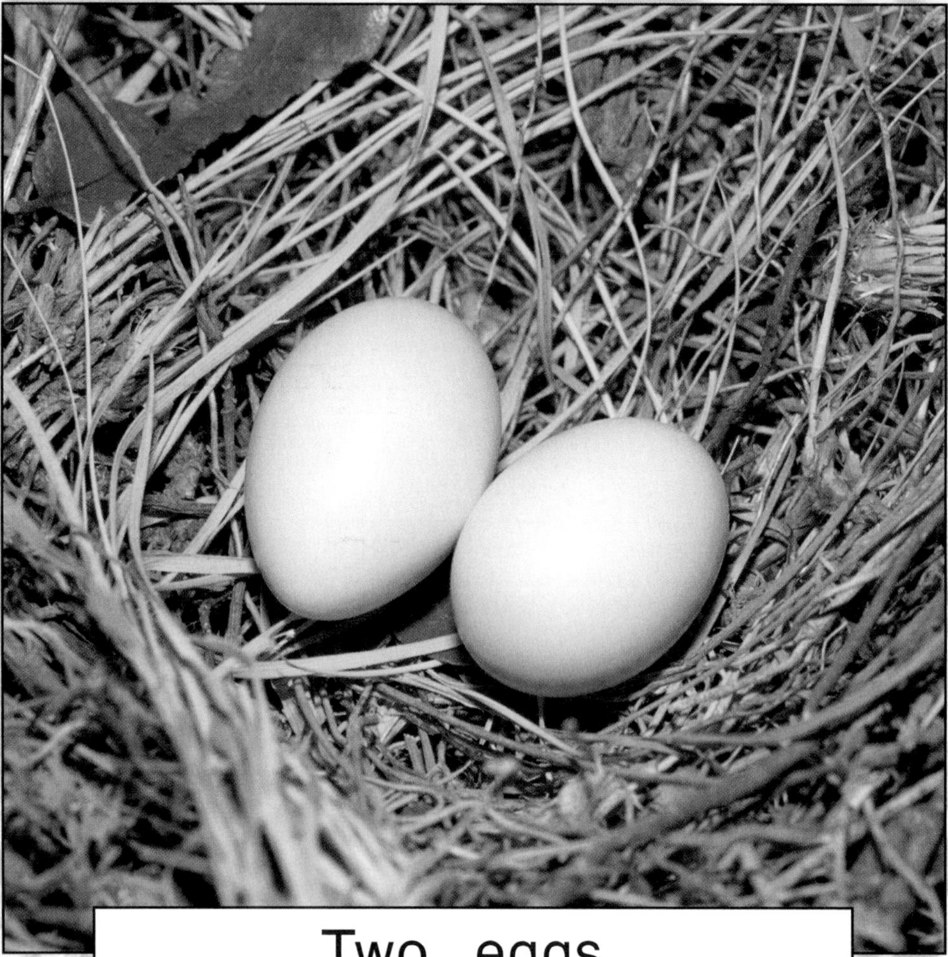

Two eggs.

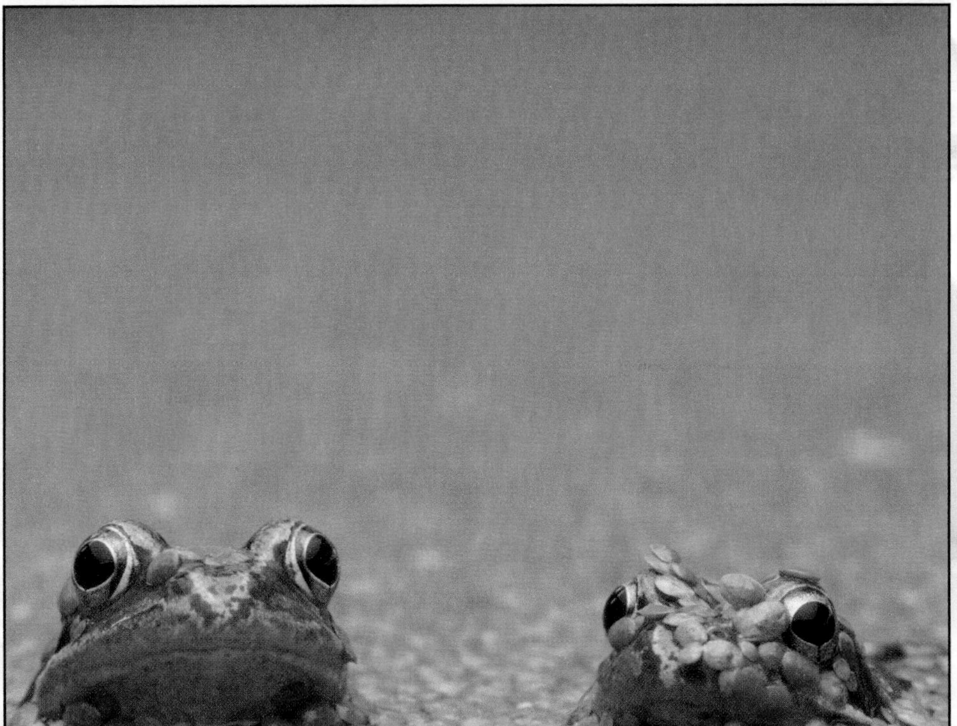

Two frogs.

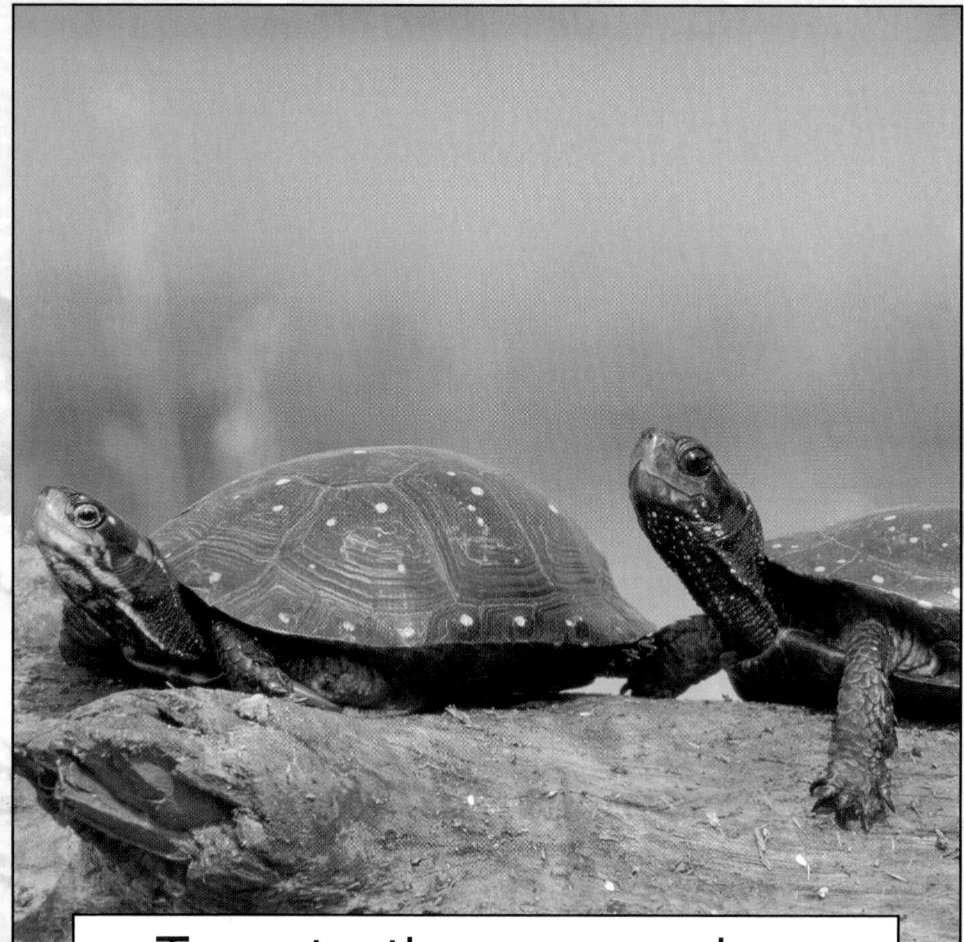

Two turtles on a log.